KU-757-260

TEACH YOURSELF BOOKS

GERMAN PHRASE BOOK

With this phrase book you need
never be at a loss when
conversing with German-speaking
people

TEACH YOURSELF BOOKS

GERMAN PHRASE
BOOK

Prepared by
JOHANNA HAMILTON, Ph.D.

TEACH YOURSELF BOOKS
ST. PAUL'S HOUSE WARWICK LANE LONDON EC4

First printed 1948
This impression 1970

ISBN 0 340 05791 2

Printed in Great Britain for The English Universities Press, Ltd.
by Richard Clay (The Chaucer Press), Ltd., Bungay, Suffolk

CONTENTS

GRAMMAR

INTRODUCTORY REMARKS

THE aim of this book is to assist the traveller in Germany, Austria and Switzerland who has no previous knowledge of the German language and enable him to meet his everyday needs and make himself understood.

The Way to Learn.—The tourist is recommended to learn the words in the following Vocabularies by heart, *repeating them aloud* with the article attached, making use of the phonetic pronunciation in the third column. In this way a large number of German words will be acquired, the gender of the nouns will be mastered, the ear familiarized with the sound of the words, and the tongue with their formation. The same plan should be followed with the Phrases.

THE PHONETIC SYSTEM

No language is written exactly as it is spelt. Although German spelling is much more regular than that of English, it will be found that the same sound is sometimes spelt in more than one way, and that the same letter may be used to represent more than one sound. In order to overcome this difficulty and to give the traveller a reliable picture of the actual pronunciation, use will be made of the phonetic script of the International Phonetic Association as given in most dictionaries of German that record the pronunciation. This consists partly of the ordinary letters of the alphabet and partly of special symbols when no letters to represent the unfamiliar sounds are available. The advantage of the system is that *each symbol represents one sound only*, and each sound is always represented by the same symbol.

Vowel Length.—The system also supplies a simple method of indicating vowel length. Short vowels receive no addition, whilst full length is indicated by a colon (:) after the vowel symbol.

Vowels are long:

(1) At the end of a syllable: **Na**me ['naːmə], except in unstressed words.

(2) When doubled: **Boo**t [boːt].

(3) When followed by *h*: **Bah**n [baːn].

(4) *i* is long when followed by *e*: **tie**f [tiːf]. But particles in an unstressed position are shortened: **die** [di], **sie** [zi].

(5) Generally before a single final consonant: **Bro**t [broːt], **Ta**t [taːt].

Vowels are short:

(1) When followed by more than one consonant: **ko**m**m**en ['kɔmən], **Kar**te ['kartə].

(2) In unstressed syllables: **be**geben [bəˈgeːbən].

9

Stress.—This is shown where necessary by a short vertical stroke (') placed *before* the stressed syllable. The principal stress falls on the first syllable of a word, e.g. **kaufen** ['kaʊfən]. The chief exceptions are :—

(1) Most foreign words, e.g. **Restaurant** [rɛstoˈrã], **probieren** [proˈbiːrən], etc.

(2) Words with the prefixes *be-, ge-, er-, ent-, ver-, zer-,* etc. which are stressed on the syllable following the prefix, e.g. **besuchen** [bəˈzuːxən], etc.

Glottal Stop (indicated by (ʔ) before the vowel).—Stressed initial vowels (and sometimes those at the beginning of the second element in a compound) are preceded by a sound called the glottal stop which is formed by closing and quickly opening the glottis, thus producing an explosive. It is like a very weak cough and is heard in English in an expression like *Jaffa oranges* (before the *o*). It is not expressed in the written language. It prevents the carrying over of a final consonant to the next syllable or word beginning with a vowel : **Der erste Tag** [der ˈʔeːrstə taːk], **Fahrkartenausgabe** [ˈfaːrkartən-ʔaʊsgaːbə].

GERMAN LETTERS WITH PHONETIC PRONUNCIATION

Vowels

Spelling.	Pronunciation.	Phonetic Symbol.
A, a	is (1) long like the *a* in *father*, e.g. **Name** [ˈnaːmə]	aː
	(2) short, as in Northern English pronunciation of *man*, when followed by two consonants, e.g. **Mann** [man]	a
E, e	is (1) a pure long vowel, as in the Northern English pronunciation of *mail*, e.g. **Mehl** [meːl], when followed by *h* or stressed	eː

Spelling.	Pronunciation.	Phonetic Symbol.

(2) as above, but shorter, in articles, e.g. **den** [den] — e

(3) open like the *e* in *pen*, when followed by *s* or two consonants, e.g. **Fest** [fɛst] and in the prefixes **er-** (ʔɛr), **ver-** (fɛr), etc. — ɛ

(4) unstressed *e* is pronounced like the *er* in *bitter* or the *a* in *China*, i.e. a murmured vowel: **bitte** [ˈbɪtə]

I, i   is (1) long like the *ee* in *meek*, e.g. **mir** [miːr] and before *e* or *h*, e.g. **fiel** [fiːl], **ihn** [ʔiːn] — iː

(2) short in unstressed **die** [di], **sie** [zi] — i

(3) short like the *i* in *if* when followed by consonants other than *r*, e.g. **mit** [mɪt], **dick** [dɪk] — ɪ

O, o   is (1) a pure long vowel, as in the Northern English pronunciation of *tone* [toːn], e.g. **Ton** [toːn] — oː

(2) short like the *o* in *not*, when followed by two consonants, e.g. **Post** [pɔst] — ɔ

U, u   is (1) long like the *oo* in English *food*, e.g. **Ruhm** [ruːm] — uː

(2) short as in English *put*, when followed by two consonants, e.g. **Fund** [fʊnt] — ʊ

Ä, ä   is (1) long and open like the *a* in *carry* lengthened, e.g. **käme** [ˈkɛːmə] — ɛː

(2) short like the *e* in *pen*, when followed by two consonants (excluding *h*), e.g. **Gäste** [ˈgɛstə] — ɛ

Ö, ö   is (1) long and like the [eː] in **Mehl** above, but with lips protruded and rounded as for whistling, e.g. **schön** [ʃøːn] — øː

Spelling.	Pronunciation.	Phonetic Symbol.
	(2) like the *e* in *pen*, but with lips protruded and rounded, when followed by two consonants, e.g. **können** ['kœnən]	œ
Ü, ü	is (1) long and like the *ee* [iː] in *see*, but with lips protruded and rounded as for whistling, e.g. **Süden** ['zyːdən]	yː
	(2) short and like the *i* in *miss*, but with lips protruded and rounded, when followed by two consonants, e.g. **müssen** ['mʏsən]	ʏ

Diphthongs

Ai, ai	is like the *i* in *mine*, e.g. **Mais** [maɪs]	aɪ
Ei, ei	,, ,, ,, ,, **fein** [faɪn]	aɪ
Au, au	,, ,, *ou* in *house*, e.g. **Haus** [haʊs]	aʊ
Äu, äu	,, ,, *oy* in *boy*, but with lip rounding throughout, **Häuser** ['hɔʏzər]	ɔʏ
Eu, eu	,, ,, *oy* in *boy*, but with lip rounding throughout, **heute** ['hɔʏtə]	ɔʏ

Vowels in French Loan Words

The vowel sounds represented by *in* in **Bassin**, *on* in **Balkon**, *an* in **Restaurant**, *um* in **Parfum** can be produced by attempting to pronounce:

in	ɛ simultaneously with ŋ : **Bassin** [ba'sɛ̃ː]			ɛ̃
on	ɔ ,, ,, ,, **Balkon** [bal'kɔ̃ː]			ɔ̃
an	a ,, ,, ,, **Restaurant** [rɛsto'rɑ̃ː]			ɑ̃
um	œ ,, ,, ,, **Parfum** [par'fœ̃ː]			œ̃

But they are often replaced by ɛŋ, ɔŋ, aŋ, œŋ

Consonants

Spelling.	Pronunciation.	Phonetic Symbol.

B, b   (1) at the beginning of a syllable is pronounced like English *b*, e.g. **Brot** [broːt]   **b**

(2) at the end of a syllable is pronounced like English *p*, e.g. **blieb** [bliːp]   **p**

C, c   (1) in isolation is used only in words of foreign origin; it is pronounced like *k*, e.g. **Café** [kaˈfeː]. (Before *e* and *i* it is now largely replaced by *Z*, e.g. **Zentimeter** for older **Centimeter**; **Zigarette** for older **Cigarette**. For pronunciation see under *Z*)   **k**

Ch, ch   (2) *c* combined with *h* has various sound values :

    (*a*) before *e* or *i* it sounds like the initial sound in English *huge*, e.g. **Chemie** [çeˈmiː], **China** [ˈçiːnaː]   **ç**

    (*b*) before other vowels or any consonant it is pronounced like *k*, e.g. **Charakter** [kaˈraktər]. Exceptions are words of French origin, in which it sounds like *sh* in *ship*, e.g. **Champagner**   **k**

    (*c*) after the sounds *a, o, u, au* it is pronounced like the *ch* in Scottish *loch*, e.g. **Bach** [bax]   **x**

    (*d*) after the vowels *e, i, ö, ü, äu, eu* and after consonants it is pronounced like the initial sound in English *huge* (see above), e.g. **brechen** [ˈbrɛçən], **mancher** [ˈmançər], **solcher** [ˈzɔlçər]

Spelling.	Pronunciation.	Phonetic Symbol.
	(e) The combination *chs* is pronounced like *ks*, e.g. **Wachs** [vaks], **sechs** [zɛks]. (Exceptions : **nächst** [nɛːçst], **höchst** [høːçst])	ks
D, d	(1) at the beginning of the word is pronounced like English *d*, e.g. **der** [deːr]	d
	(2) at the end of a syllable is pronounced like English *t*, e.g. **Rad** [raːt]; *dt* is pronounced like *t*, e.g. **Stadt** [stat]	t
F, f	is pronounced like English *f* in *father*, e.g. **frei** [fraɪ], **laufen** [ˈlaʊfən]	f
G, g	(1) at the beginning of a syllable is pronounced like English *g*, e.g. **gut** [guːt]	g
	(2) at the end of a syllable after *a, e, o, u* is pronounced like English *k*, e.g. **Tag** [taːk]. (The pronunciation x like the *ch* in Scottish *loch* is often heard in North Germany, e.g. **Zug** [tsuːx])	k
	(3) at the end of a syllable after *i* is pronounced like the initial sound in English *huge*, e.g. **Honig** [ˈhoːnɪç]	ç
H, h	(1) at the beginning of a syllable is pronounced like English *h* in *house*, e.g. **Haus** [haʊs], **Schönheit** [ˈʃøːnhaɪt]	h
	(2) is not pronounced after vowels nor after *t*, e.g. **Schuh** [ʃuː], **Theater** [teˈʔaːtər]	
J, j	represents the same sound as the *y* in *year*, e.g. **Jahr** [jaːr]	j
K, k	is pronounced like English *k*, e.g. **Karte** [ˈkartə]	k
L, l	is always pronounced like the initial English *l* in *long*, e.g. **lang** [laŋ], **hell** [hɛl]	l
M, m	is pronounced like English *m* in *must*, e.g. **müssen** [ˈmʏsən], **kommen** [ˈkɔmən]	m

Spelling.		Pronunciation.	Phonetic Symbol.
N, n		is pronounced like English *n* in *night*, e.g. Nacht [naxt], brennen [ˈbrɛnən]	n
	ng	has the same quality as the *ng* in *singer*, e.g. Finger [ˈfɪŋər], eng [ɛŋ]	ŋ
P, p		is pronounced like English *p* in *post*, e.g. Post [pɔst], Suppe [ˈzʊpə]	p
Pf, pf		is pronounced as it is written, e.g. Pfund [pfʊnt], Topf [tɔpf]	pf
Ph, ph		is pronounced like English *ph*, e.g. Photograph [fotoˈgraːf]	f
Qu, qu		is pronounced *kv*, thus differing in its second element from the English *qu* in *quick*, e.g. Quelle [ˈkvɛlə]	kv
R, r		is pronounced differently in different parts of Germany, either as the *uvular r* (produced by the vibration of the uvula) resembling the French *r*, or as the *lingual r* (produced by the vibration of the tip of the tongue against the upper gum), e.g. Reise [ˈraɪzə], Karte [ˈkartə]	r
S, s		is pronounced like the *z* in *zero* at the beginning of a syllable before a vowel, e.g. sein [zaɪn], besuchen [bəˈzuːxən]; it is always like the English *s* in *sing* at the end of a syllable, e.g. das [das], deshalb [ˈdeshalp]	z s
	ss	is always pronounced like *ss* in *hiss*, e.g. Wasser [ˈvasər], Fuss [fuːs]	s
Sch, sch		is pronounced like English *sh* in *shoe*, e.g. Schuh [ʃuː]	ʃ
Sp, sp St, st		are pronounced like *shp* and *sht* when they stand at the beginning of a syllable, e.g. Sprache [ˈʃpraːxə], versprechen [fɛrˈʃprɛçən], Stadt [ʃtat], bestellen [bəˈʃtɛlən]	ʃp ʃt

Spelling.	Pronunciation.	Phonetic Symbol.
T, t	is pronounced like *t* in *ten*, e.g. **Tat** [taːt]	t
V, v	represents the same sound as *f* in *father*, e.g. **Vater** [ˈfaːtər], **von** [fɔn]	f
W, w	is the same sound as the English *v* in *very*, e.g. **Wetter** [ˈvɛtər]	v
X, x	is pronounced like English *x* in *fox*, e.g. **Axt** [akst]	ks
Z, z	is pronounced like English *ts* in *cats*, e.g. **zehn** [tseːn]	ts

KEY TO THE PHONETIC SYMBOLS

Vowels

Long

			Nearest equivalent in :	
			English.	French.
iː	Biene	[ˈbiːnə]	b*ee*	
eː	Erde	[ˈʔeːrdə]		f*é*e
ɛː	Fähre	[ˈfɛːrə]		p*è*re
aː	Pfad	[pfaːt]	p*a*th	
oː	rot	[roːt]		m*o*t
uː	Schule	[ˈʃuːlə]	sch*oo*l	
yː	Süden	[ˈzyːdən]		s*u*d
øː	schön	[ʃøːn]		h*eu*r*eu*x
ɛ̃ː	Bassin	[baˈsɛ̃ː]		bass*in*
ɑ̃ː	lancieren	[lɑ̃ːˈsiːrən]		l*an*cer
ɔ̃ː	Balkon	[balˈkɔ̃ː]		balc*on*
œ̃ː	Parfum	[parˈfœ̃ː]		parf*um*

Short

			Nearest equivalent in:	
			English.	French.
ɪ	in	[ʔɪn]	*in*	
e	der	[der]		*été*
ɛ	setzen	[ˈzɛtsən]	s*e*t	
*ə	gegeben	[gəˈgeːbən]	gi*v*en	
ɔ	kommen	[ˈkɔmən]	b*o*ttom	
a	fallen	[ˈfalən]		b*a*l
ʊ	Butter	[ˈbʊtər]	p*u*sh	
œ	können	[ˈkœnən]		pl*eu*rer
ʏ	müssen	[ˈmʏsən]		s*u*pposer

* Only in unstressed syllables.

Diphthongs

aɪ	Stein	[ʃtaɪn]
aʊ	Haus	[haʊs]
ɔʏ	heute	[ˈhɔʏtə]

Consonants

p	Post	[pɔst]
b	Brot	[broːt]
t	Tasse	[ˈtasə]
d	Dampf	[dampf]
k	Karte	[ˈkartə]
g	gut	[guːt]
ʔ	Haupteingang	[ˈhaʊptʔaɪngaŋ]
m	Marke	[ˈmarkə]
n	nur	[nuːr]
ŋ	Ring	[rɪŋ]
l	leben	[ˈleːbən]
r	Reise	[ˈraɪzə]
f	Fahrt	[faːrt]
v	wer	[veːr]
s	besser	[ˈbɛsər]
z	sagen	[ˈzaːgən]

ʃ	schwer	[ʃveːr]
ʒ	Etage	[ʔeˈtaːʒə]
ç	ich	[ʔɪç]
j	Jahr	[jaːr]
x	machen	[ˈmaxən], suchen [ˈzuːxən]
h	Halle	[ˈhalə]
ĭ	Emilie	[ʔeˈmiːlĭə] (semi-vowel)
ŭ	Statue	[ˈʃtaːtŭə] „

An outline of German grammar has been added at the end of the book for the benefit of those who wish to study the language in more detail.

THE
PHRASE BOOK

PASSPORT FORMALITIES
(PASSFORMALITÄTEN)

Before going abroad, the traveller must obtain a passport.
When a person arrives at the German frontier, he has to pro-
duce his passport, and the date of entry is stamped in it.
Further particulars as to visas, permits for a lengthy stay, etc.
may be obtained from the Passport Office, Clive House, Petty
France, S.W.1. A passport may be obtained from the local
office of the Ministry of Labour, Employment Exchange.

A very useful address for travellers seeking information is
the German Tourist Information Bureau, 6 Vigo Street,
Regent Street, London, W.1, which represents the German
Central Tourist Association in the United Kingdom.

At the moment a visa is not necessary to enter Germany
unless one intends to stay longer than three months. The
visa can be obtained from the German Consulate, 43 Wilton
Crescent, S.W.7.

Vocabulary

English.	German.	Pronunciation.
The passport	der Pass	der pas
The passport examination	die Passkontrolle	di ˈpaskɔnˈtrɔlə
The visa	das Visum	das ˈviːzʊm
	der Sichtvermerk	der ˈziçtfərˈmɛrk
The travel visa	das Reisevisum	das ˈraɪzəˈviːzʊm
The journey of entry	die Einreise	di ˈʔaɪnraɪzə
The exit journey	die Ausreise	di ˈʔaʊsraɪzə
The stay	der Aufenthalt	der ˈʔaʊfənthalt
The permit to stay	die Aufenthalts-erlaubnis	di ˈʔaʊfənthalts-ʔerˈlaʊpnis
The purpose	der Zweck	der tsvɛk
The fee	die Gebühren	di gəˈbyːrən

21

Phrases

English.	German and Pronunciation.
Do I need a visa?	Brauche ich ein Visum (einen 'brauxə ʔɪç ʔaɪn 'viːzʊm 'ʔaɪnən Sichtvermerk)? 'zɪçtfɛr'mɛrk?
I am going as a tourist	Ich reise als Tourist ʔɪç 'raɪzə ʔals tu'rɪst
I wish to seek employment	Ich suche Arbeit (Beschäftigung) ʔɪç 'zuːxə 'ʔarbaɪt bə'ʃɛftɪɡʊŋ
I am travelling through Germany	Ich bin auf der Durchreise ʔɪç bɪn ʔauf der 'dʊrçraɪzə
I wish to break the journey	Ich möchte die Reise unterbrechen ʔɪç 'mœçtə di 'raɪzə ʔʊntər'brɛçən
How long may I stay in the country?	Wie lange kann ich im Lande viː 'laŋə kan ʔɪç ʔɪm 'landə bleiben? 'blaɪbən?
Do I report to the police?	Muss ich mich bei der Polizei mʊs ʔɪç mɪç baɪ der poli'tsaɪ melden? 'mɛldən?
How much does the visa cost?	Was kostet das Visum? vas 'kɔstət das 'viːzʊm?
Must I get a permit to stay (to take up work)?	Brauche ich eine Aufenthalts- 'brauxə ʔɪç 'ʔaɪnə 'ʔaufənthalts- erlaubnis (wenn ich Arbeit ʔɛr'laupnɪs (vɛn ʔɪç 'ʔarbaɪt annehme)? 'ʔanneːmə?
You must have your passport renewed	Sie müssen Ihren Pass erneuern zi 'mʏsən 'ʔiːrən pas ʔɛr'nɔyərn lassen 'lasən
Where is the British Consulate?	Wo ist das Britische Konsulat? voː ʔɪst das 'brɪtɪʃə kɔnzu'laːt?

CUSTOMS (ZOLL)
Vocabulary

English.	German.	Pronunciation.
The duty (customs)	der Zoll	der tsɔl
The custom-house	das Zollamt	das ˈtsɔlʔamt
The customs officer	der Zollbeamte	der ˈtsɔlbəʔamtə
The luggage	das Gepäck	das gəˈpɛk
The tobacco	der Tabak	der ˈtaːbak
The cigar	die Zigarre	di tsiˈgarə
The coffee	der Kaffee	der ˈkafeː
The tea	der Tee	der teː
The perfume	das Parfum	das parˈfœ̃ː
The camera	der Photographen-apparat	der fotoˈgraːfən-ʔapaˈraːt
	die Kamera	di ˈkaːməra
The dutiable articles	zollpflichtige Waren (Gegenstände, Artikel)	ˈtsɔlflɪçtɪgə ˈvaːrən (ˈgeːgən-ˈstɛndə, ʔarˈtikəl)

Phrases

English.	German and Pronunciation.
Where is the custom-house?	Wo ist das Zollamt? voː ʔist das ˈtsɔlʔamt?
Here is my luggage	Hier ist mein Gepäck hiːr ʔist main gəˈpɛk
Will you examine my luggage?	Wollen Sie mein Gepäck untersuchen? ˈvɔlən zi main gəˈpɛk ʔuntərˈzuːxən?
Have you anything to declare?	Haben Sie etwas zu verzollen? ˈhaːbən zi ˈʔɛtvas tsu fɛrˈtsɔlən?
Have you any of the articles on the list?	Haben Sie einen der (auf der Liste) verzeichneten Gegenstände? ˈhaːbən zi ˈʔainən deːr ʔauf der ˈlistə fɛrˈtsaiçnətən ˈgeːgən-ˈʃtɛndə?

English.	German and Pronunciation.
Have you any spirits or tobacco?	**Haben Sie Alkohol oder Tabak?** ˈhaːbən zi ˈʔalkohɔl ˈʔoːdər ˈtaːbak?
I have this small bottle of perfume	**Ich habe diese kleine Flasche Parfüm** ʔɪç ˈhaːbə ˈdiːzə ˈklaɪnə ˈflaʃə parˈfœ̃ː
That is free of duty	**Das ist zollfrei** das ʔɪst ˈtsɔlfraɪ
Is that all?	**Ist das alles?** ʔɪst das ˈʔaləs?
Is my luggage passed?	**Ist mein Gepäck durchgelassen?** ʔɪst maɪn gəˈpɛk ˈdʊrçgəlasən?
Will you take this luggage to a taxi?	**Bringen Sie dieses Gepäck zur Taxe (bitte)!** ˈbriŋən zi ˈdiːzəs gəˈpɛk tsʊr takse ˈbɪtə!

TRAVEL BY RAIL AND ROAD (LANDREISEN)

A. *Travelling by Rail* (Mit der Bahn, Eisenbahn, reisen)

The railways in Germany are owned and run by the State (**Bundesbahn**). There are several types of trains : besides the long-distance corridor or express trains called **D-Züge** and **F-Züge,** which stop at very few stations, there are the slow local trains (**Personenzüge**). An intermediate type of moderately fast train is called **Eilzug.** Express diesel railcars (**Triebwagen**) are being increasingly used on the long distance routes, as are rail buses (**Schienenomnibusse**) on the secondary lines.

There is a surcharge (**Zuschlag**) for express trains. Seats can be reserved on the trains (**Platzkarte**) at the station of departure.

Trains have only two classes: **Erste Klasse** (carriages with upholstered seats) and **Zweite Klasse** (with wooden seats), but most long-distance trains and many local trains have upholstered seats in the second class. The same restaurant car is open to both classes. Corridor trains can only be entered by a door at each end of the coach.

Suburban lines (**Vorortbahnen**) and metropolitan lines (**Stadtbahnen**) are mostly electric.

Vocabulary

English.	German.	Pronunciation.
The transport	das Verkehrsmittel	das fɛrˈkeːrsmɪtəl
The railway	die Eisenbahn, die Bahn	di ˈʔaɪzənˈbaːn, diː baːn
The station	der Bahnhof	der ˈbaːnhoːf
The train	der Zug	der tsuːk
The enquiry office	die Auskunft	di ˈʔaʊskʊnft
The ticket	die Fahrkarte	di ˈfaːrkartə
The booking-office	der Fahrkarten- schalter	der ˈfaːrkartən- ˈʃaltər
The fare	das Fahrgeld	das ˈfaːrgɛlt
The platform	der Bahnsteig	der ˈbaːnʃtaɪk
The express train	der Schnellzug	der ˈʃnɛltsuːk
The slow train	der Personenzug	der pɛrˈzoːnən- ˈtsuːk
The coach, carriage	der Wagen	der ˈvaːgən
The through-carriage	der Kurswagen	der ˈkʊrsvaːgən
The compartment	das Abteil	das ˈʔaptaɪl
The seat	der Sitzplatz	der ˈzɪtsplats
The corner seat	der Eckplatz	der ˈʔɛkplats
To reserve a seat	einen Platz belegen	ˈʔaɪnən plats bəˈleːgən
The lavatory	die Toilette, der Abort	di toaˈlɛtə, der ˈʔapʔɔrt
The passenger	der Fahrgast	der ˈfaːrgast
The luggage	das Gepäck	das gəˈpɛk
The cloak-room	die Gepäckaufbewah- rung(-sstelle)	di gəˈpɛkʔauf- bəvaːruŋsˈʃtɛlə
The arrival	die Ankunft	di ˈʔankʊnft
The departure	die Abfahrt	di ˈʔapfaːrt
The barrier	die Sperre	di ˈʃpɛrə
The escalator	die Rolltreppe	di ˈrɔltrɛpə

Phrases

English.	German and Pronunciation.
Where do I get a ticket?	Wo löse ich mir eine Fahrkarte? voː ˈløːzə ʔɪç miːr ˈʔaɪnə ˈfaːrkartə?

English.	German and Pronunciation.
Is the booking-office open?	Ist der Fahrkartenschalter geöffnet? ˀɪst der ˈfaːrkartən|ʃaltər gəˀˀœfnət?
One second return Berlin for the express 6.10, and a platform ticket	Eine Rückfahrkarte zweiter Klasse ˈˀaɪnə ˈrʏkfaːrˈkartə ˈtsvaɪtər ˈklasə nach Berlin für den Schnellzug naːx bərˈliːn fyːr den ˈʃnɛltsuːk sechs Uhr zehn und eine Bahn-ˈzɛks ˀuːr ˈtseːn ˀʊnt ˀˀaɪnə ˈbaːn-steigkarte ʃtaɪkˈkartə
Are you travelling via Leipzig or Halle?	Fahren Sie über Leipzig oder ˈfaːrən zi ˈˀyːbər ˈlaɪptsɪç ˈˀoːdər Halle? ˈhalə?
Which is the shortest way?	Welches ist die kürzeste Strecke? ˈvɛlçəs ˀɪst di ˈkʏrtsəstə ˈʃtrɛkə?
What is the fare to Berlin?	Was kostet eine Fahrkarte nach vas ˈkɔstət ˀˀaɪnə ˈfaːrkartə naːx Berlin? bərˈliːn?
You have to pay a surcharge on this ticket	Sie müssen eine Zuschlagskarte zi ˈmʏsən ˈˀaɪnə ˈtsuːʃlaːksˈkartə lösen ˈløːzən
Have your change ready	Das Fahrgeld ist abgezählt bereit das ˈfaːrgɛlt ˀɪst ˈˀapgətseːlt bəˈraɪt zu halten! tsu ˈhaltən!
Can I break the journey?	Kann ich die Fahrt unterbrechen? kan ˀɪç di faːrt ˀʊntərˈbrɛxən?
Shall I get the connection?	Werde ich den Anschluss erreichen? ˈveːrdə ˀɪç den ˈˀanʃlus ˀɛrˈraɪçən?
Where must I change?	Wo muss ich umsteigen? ˈvoː mus ˀɪç ˈˀʊmʃtaɪgən?
Will the train be late?	Hat der Zug Verspätung? hat der tsuːk fɛrˈʃpɛːtung?

English.	German and Pronunciation.
Porter, please register this luggage to Munich	Gepäckträger, (bitte) geben Sie dies gə'pɛktrɛːgər 'bɪtə 'geːbən zi diːs Gepäck nach München auf ! gə'pɛk naːx 'mʏnçən ʔauf !
You will have to pay excess luggage on this	Sie müssen darauf Übergewicht zi 'mʏsən da'rauf 'ʔyːbərgəvɪçt bezahlen bə'tsaːlən
Please bring me the registration slip to the 1st Class restaurant	(Bitte), bringen Sie mir den Gepäck- 'bɪtə 'brɪŋən zi miːr den gə'pɛk schein in den Wartesaal I. ʃaɪn ʔɪn den 'vartə'zaːl 'ʔeːrstər Klasse! 'klasə!
Please leave these suitcases in the cloakroom	(Bitte), geben Sie diese Handkoffer in 'bɪtə 'geːbən zi 'diːzə 'hantkɔfər ʔɪn der Gepäckuefbewahrungsstelle ab! der gə'pɛkʔaufbəva:ruŋs'ʃtɛlə ʔap!
From which platform does the train start?	Von welchem Bahnsteig fährt der fɔn 'vɛlçem 'baːnʃtaɪk fɛːrt der Zug ab? tsuːk ʔap?
Platform No. IV through the subway	Bahnsteig Nummer vier durch die 'baːnʃtaɪk 'nʊmər fiːr dʊrç di Unterführung ʔʊntər'fyːruŋ
Please get me a corner seat first class, facing the engine, non-smoker	Besorgen Sie mir (bitte) einen bə'zɔrgən zi miːr bɪtə 'ʔaɪnən Eckplatz erster Klasse, vorwärts, 'ʔɛkplats 'ʔeːrstər 'klasə 'fɔrvɛrts Nichtraucher (abteil) ! 'nɪçtrauxər 'ʔaptaɪl !
Is there a restaurant car on the train?	Ist ein Speisewagen im Zug? ʔɪst ʔaɪn 'ʃpaɪzə'vaːgən ʔɪm tsuːk ?
This train is entirely a sleeper	Dieser Zug führt nur Schlafwagen 'diːzər tsuːk fyːrt nuːr 'ʃlaːfvaːgən

English.	German and Pronunciation.
Have you a reserved seat ?	Haben Sie einen Platz belegt ?
	'ha:bən zi 'ʔaɪnən plats bə'le:kt ?
When does the train arrive ?	Wann kommt der Zug an ?
	van kɔmt der tsu:k ʔan ?
You will find the arrival and departure times of the trains in the railway guide	Ankunft und Abfahrt der Züge
	'ʔankunft ʔunt 'ʔapfa:rt der 'tsy:gə
	sind im Kursbuch zu finden
	zɪnt ʔɪm 'kursbu:x tsu 'fɪndən
Here is the summer time-table	Hier ist der Sommerfahrplan
	hi:r ʔɪst der 'zɔmər'fa:rpla:n
I bought my ticket at the travel agency	Ich habe meine Karte (Fahrkarte)
	ʔiç 'ha:bə 'maɪnə 'kartə ('fa:rkartə)
	im Reisebüro gekauft
	ʔɪm 'raɪzəby'ro: gə'kauft
Have you insured your luggage ?	Haben Sie Ihr Reisegepäck versichert ?
	'ha:bən zi ʔi:r 'raɪzəgə'pɛk fɛrzɪçərt ?
Take your seats, please	Alle einsteigen !
	'ʔalə 'ʔaɪnʃtaɪgən !
Your case is too large for the luggage rack	Ihr Koffer ist zu gross für das Gepäcknetz
	ʔi:r 'kɔfər ʔɪst tsu: gro:s fy:r das gə'pɛknɛts
Windows may only be opened with the permission of all fellow passengers	Die Fenster dürfen nur mit Zustimmung aller Mitreisenden geöffnet werden
	di 'fɛnstər 'dʏrfən nu:r mɪt 'tsu:ʃtɪmuŋ 'ʔalər 'mɪtraɪzəndən gə'ʔœfnət 've:rdən
Do not lean out of the window	Nicht hinauslehnen !
	nɪçt hɪ'nausle:nən !
Where is the emergency signal ?	Wo ist die Notbremse ?
	'vo: ʔɪst di 'no:tbrɛmzə ?
Which is the next station ?	Welches ist die nächste Station ?
	'vɛlçəs ʔɪst di 'nɛ:çstə ʃtatsɪ'o:n ?

English.	German and Pronunciation.
How long do we stop here ?	**Wie lange haben wir hier Aufent-** vi: ˈlaŋə ˈhaːbən viːr hiːr ˈʔaufənt- **halt ?** halt ?
You had better ask the ticket-collector when he checks the tickets	**Fragen Sie lieber den Schaffner,** ˈfraːgən zi ˈliːbər den ˈʃafnər **wenn er die Fahrkarten revidiert** vɛn ʔer dɪ ˈfaːrkartən reviˈdiːrt
Munich ! All change here	**München ! Alle aussteigen !** ˈmʏnçən ! ˈʔalə ˈʔausʃtaɪgən !
I have left my overcoat in the train. Where is the Lost Property Office ?	**Ich habe meinen Mantel im Zug** ʔɪç ˈhaːbə ˈmaɪnən ˈmantəl ʔɪm tsuːk **hängen lassen, wo ist das Fund-** ˈhɛŋən ˈlasən, voː ʔɪst das ˈfunt- **büro?** byˈroː?
Where is the station hotel ?	**Wo ist das Bahnhofshotel ?** voː ʔɪst das ˈbaːnhoːfshoˈtɛl ?

B. Travelling by Car (Mit dem Auto reisen)

Since the construction of the **Reichsautobahnen** covering Germany with a network of high-class motor-roads a great impetus has been given to travelling by car. These **Reichsautobahnen** are divided by a green belt in the middle and are very wide. Owing to their straight course they are sometimes carried over valleys by bridges, enabling motorists to travel with great speed, the more so as provision is made for overtaking cars travelling at slow speed. Another feature is that **Autobahnen** are carried on viaducts over those running at right angles, thus avoiding crossings, slowing up, and danger of collision.

Vocabulary

English.	German.	Pronunciation.
The motor-car	**das Auto, das Automobil der Wagen**	das ˈʔautoɪ, das ʔautoˈbiːl der ˈvaːgən

English.	German.	Pronunciation.
The motor bus (coach)	der Autobus	der ˈꝯautobʊs
The charabanc	das Verkehrsauto	das fɛrˈkeːrsꝯautoː
The taxi(cab)	die Taxe	di takse
The motorist	der Autofahrer	der ˈꝯautoˈfaːrər
The motor-cycle	das Motorrad	das ˈmoːtorraːt
The motor-scooter	der Motorroller	der ˈmoːtorˈrɔlər
The chassis	das Fahrgestell	das ˈfaːrgəˈʃtɛl
The body	die Karosserie	di karɔsəˈriː
The bonnet	die Haube	di ˈhaubə
The mudguard	der Kotflügel	der ˈkoːtflyːgəl
The wheel	das Rad	das raːt
The tyre	der Reifen	der ˈraɪfən
The brake	die Bremse	di ˈbrɛmzə
The gear-lever	der Schalthebel	der ˈʃaltheːbəl
The gear-box	das Getriebe	das gəˈtriːbə
The steering wheel	das Steuerrad	das ˈʃtɔyərˈraːt
The exhaust	der Auspuff	der ˈꝯauspuf
The battery	die Batterie	di batəˈriː
The carburettor	der Vergaser	der fɛrˈgaːzər
The accelerator	der Gashebel	der ˈgaːsheːbəl
The bumper	die Stossstange	di ˈʃtoːsʃtaŋə
The motor-horn	die Hupe	di ˈhuːpə
The wind-screen	die Windschutz- scheibe	di ˈvɪntʃuts- ˈʃaɪbə
The spare parts	die Ersatzteile	di ꝯɛrˈzatstaɪlə
The petrol station	die Tankstelle	di ˈtaŋkʃtɛlə
The petrol	das Benzin, der Treibstoff	das bɛnˈtsiːn, deːr ˈtraɪpʃtɔf
The garage (for re- pairs)	die Wagenpflege (die Reparatur- werkstätte)	di ˈvaːgənpflegə (diː reparaˈtuːr- vɛrkˈʃtɛtə)
To overtake	überholen	ꝯyːbərˈhoːlən

Phrases

English.	German and Pronunciation.
What is the horse-power of your car?	**Wieviel Pferdekräfte hat Ihr** ˈviːfiːl ˈpfeɪrdəˈkrɛftə hat ʔiːr **Auto?** ˈʔautoɪ?
My car is a two-seater	**Mein Auto ist ein Zweisitzer** maɪn ˈʔautoɪ ʔɪst ʔaɪn ˈtsvaɪzɪtsər
Who will drive to-day?	**Wer will heute das Auto** veɪr vɪl ˈhɔytə das ˈautoɪ **fahren** ˈfaɪrən
Have you got your driving licence with you?	**Haben Sie Ihren Führerschein bei** ˈhaːbən zi ˈʔiːrən ˈfyːrərˈʃaɪn baɪ **sich?** zɪç?
Hadn't we better let the hood down? it's getting hot	**Wollen wir nicht lieber das Verdeck** ˈvɔlən viːr nɪçt ˈliːbər das fɛrˈdɛk **aufklappen? es wird heiss (warm)** ˈʔaufklapən? ʔɛs vɪrt haɪs (varm)
Look out for the bends, otherwise we shall skid	**Vorsicht bei den Kurven, sonst** ˈfoːrzɪçt baɪ den ˈkurvən zɔnst **schleudert der Wagen** ˈʃlɔydərt der ˈvaːgən
Did you see the traffic lights?	**Haben Sie die Verkehrsampeln** ˈhaːbən zi di fɛrˈkeːrsʔampəln **(-lichter) gesehen?** (-ˈlɪçtər) gəˈzeːən?
The traffic policeman took our number	**Der Verkehrsschutzmann hat uns** der fɛrˈkeːrsˈʃutsman hat ʔuns **aufgeschrieben** ˈʔaufgəʃriːbən

English.	German and Pronunciation.
We shall have to pay a fine	Wir werden Ordnungsstrafe viːr ˈveːrdən ˈˀɔrdnuŋsˈʃtraɪfə bezahlen müssen bəˈtsaɪlən ˈmʏsən
I had a break-down on my journey	Ich hatte unterwegs eine Panne ˀɪç ˈhatə ˀʊntərˈveɪks ˈˀaɪnə ˈpanə
It does not matter if we get a puncture, I have a spare wheel with me	Es schadet nichts, wenn wir Reifen- ˀɛs ˈʃaɪdət nɪçts vɛn viːr ˈraɪfən- panne haben (ein Reifen panə ˈhaːbən (ˀaɪn ˈraɪfən platzt), ich habe ein Reserverad platst) ˀɪç ˈhaːbə ˀaɪn reˈzɛrvəˈraɪt mit mɪt
Have you any spare parts with you?	Haben Sie ein paar Ersatzteile bei ˈhaːbən zi ˀaɪn paːr ˀɛrˈzatstaɪlə baɪ sich? zɪç?
Shall I press the self-starter?	Soll ich den Anlasser in Gang zɔl ˀɪç den ˈˀanlasər ˀɪn gaŋ bringen? ˈbrɪŋən?
Step on the gas	Gib Gas ! giːp gaːs !
You must switch on the headlights	Sie müssen den Scheinwerfer ein- zi ˈmʏsən den ˈʃaɪnvɛrfər ˈˀaɪn- schalten ʃaltən
Shall I start the screen-wiper?	Soll ich den Scheibenwischer zɔl ˀɪç den ˈʃaɪbənˈvɪʃər benutzen bəˈnutsən?
I must change into second gear	Ich muss den zweiten Gang ein- ˀɪç mʊs ·den ˈtsvaɪtən gaŋ ˈˀaɪn- schalten ʃaltən

English.	German and Pronunciation.
We are going downhill	**Wir fahren bergab** viːr ˈfaːrən bɛrkˈʔap
Where can I park (my car)?	**Wo kann ich (meinen Wagen) parken?** voː kan ʔɪç ˈmaɪnən ˈvaːgən ˈparkən?
Where can I get this car repaired? I have had a collision	**Wo kann ich dieses Auto reparieren lassen? Ich hatte einen Zusammenstoss** voɪ kan ʔɪç diːzəs ˈʔautoɪ repaˈriːrən ˈlasən? ʔɪç ˈhatə ˈʔaɪnən tsuˈzamənˈʃtoɪs
Where is the nearest petrol station?	**Wo ist die nächste Tankstelle?** voː ʔɪst di ˈnɛːçstə ˈtaŋkʃtɛlə?
I must get my tank filled and have my tyres inflated	**Ich muss tanken und meine Reifen aufpumpen lassen** ʔɪç mus ˈtaŋkən ʔunt ˈmaɪnə ˈraɪfən ˈʔaufpumpən ˈlasən
Slow down	**Langsam fahren!** ˈlaŋzaːm ˈfaːrən!
One-way road	**Einbahnstrasse!** ˈʔaɪnbaːnˈʃtraːsə!
Speed limit eighty kilometres	**Höchstgeschwindigkeit achtzig km.** ˈhøɪçstgəˈʃvɪndɪçkaɪt ˈʔaxtsɪç kiloˈmeɪtər
Beware of the crossroads	**Achtung! Strassenkreuzung!** ˈʔaxtuŋ! ˈʃtraːsənˈkrɔʏtsuŋ!
Main road ahead	**Achtung! Hauptverkehrsstrasse!** ˈʔaxtuŋ! hauptvɛrˈkeɪrsʃtraɪsə!
Level crossing	**Bahnübergang** ˈbaɪnʔyˈbərgaŋ
Road repairs. Diversion	**Achtung! Baustelle, Umleitung!** ˈʔaxtuŋ! ˈbauʃtɛlə, ˈʔumlaɪtuŋ!
Heed right of way	**Vorfahrt achten!** ˈfoɪrfaɪrt ˈʔaxtən

B (GER. PHR.)

TRAVELLING BY BOAT (SEEREISEN)

There are only two coastal areas in Germany, that of the North Sea and the Baltic. The big North Sea ports such as Hamburg and Bremen are the starting-points for trans-ocean voyages, such as that to America. As both Hamburg and Bremen are situated a considerable distance up rivers (Elbe and Weser) the largest passenger ships start from the ports of Cuxhaven and Bremerhaven. There are usually three classes (**Erste Klasse, zweite Klasse, Zwischendeck**—steerage).

Vocabulary

English.	German.	Pronunciation.
The port, harbour	**der Hafen**	der 'haːfən
The steamship company	**die Schiffahrtsgesell-schaft**	di 'ʃ-ffaːrtsgə'zɛl-ʃaft
The liner	**der Passagierdamp-fer, das Fahrgast-schiff**	der pasa'ʒiːrdamp-fər, das 'faːrgast-'ʃif
The mono-class liner, the inter-mediate liner	**der Einheitsdamp-fer, der Touristen-dampfer**	der 'ʔainhaits-'dampfər, der tu'ristən'dampfər
The first class	**erste Klasse**	'ʔeːrstə 'klasə
The steerage	**das Zwischendeck**	das 'tsviʃən'dɛk
The passage, cross-ing	**die Überfahrt**	di 'ʔyːbər'faːrt
The hull	**der Schiffsrumpf**	der 'ʃifsrumpf
The bow	**der Bug**	der buːk
The stern	**das Heck**	das hɛk
The gangway	**der Schiffssteg**	der 'ʃifsʃteːk
The funnel	**der Schornstein**	der 'ʃɔrnʃtain
The porthole	**das Bullauge**	das 'bulʔaugə
The railings	**die Reeling**	di 'reːliŋ
The mast	**der Mast**	der mast
The dining-saloon	**der Speisesaal**	der 'ʃpaizəzaːl
The smoking-room	**das Rauchzimmer**	das 'rauxtsimər

English.	German.	Pronunciation.
The cabin	die Kabine	di ka'bi:nə
The deck	das Deck	das dɛk
The deck-chair	der Liegestuhl	der 'li:gə'ʃtu:l
The life-boat	das Rettungsboot	das 'rɛtuŋs'bo:t
The life-belt	der Rettungsring	der 'rɛtuŋs'rɪŋ
The passenger	der Fahrgast	der 'fa:rgast
The seasickness	die Seekrankheit	di 'ze:kraŋkhaɪt
The crew	die Besatzung	di bə'zatsuŋ
The captain	der Kapitän	der kapi'tɛ:n
The purser	der Zahlmeister	der 'tsa:lmaɪstər
To book the passage	die Schiffskarte lösen	di 'ʃɪfskartə 'lø:zən
To embark	an Bord gehen, sich einschiffen	ʔan bɔrt 'ge:ən, zɪç 'ʔaɪnʃɪfən
To disembark	sich ausschiffen, landen	ɛɪç 'ʔausʃɪfən, 'landən
To roll	schlingern	'ʃlɪŋərn
To pitch	stampfen	'ʃtampfən

Phrases

English.	German and Pronunciation.
Have you taken your steamer ticket?	Haben Sie Ihre Schiffskarte gelöst? 'ha:bən zi 'ʔi:rə 'ʃɪfskartə gə'lø:st?
Which route are you travelling?	Welche Route fahren Sie? 'vɛlçə 'ru:tə 'fa:rən zi?
When are you sailing?	Wann fahren Sie ab? van 'fa:rən zi ʔap?
I am travelling first class	Ich fahre erster Klasse ʔɪç 'faɪrə 'ʔeɪrstər 'klasə
This cargo boat (freighter) takes passengers too	Dieser Frachtdampfer (Frachter) 'di:zər 'fraxtdampfər ('fraxtər) nimmt auch Fahrgäste mit nɪmt ʔaux 'fa:rgɛstə mɪt
How many knots does she do?	Wieviele Knoten fährt er? vɪ'fi:lə 'kno:tən fɛ:rt ʔer?

English.	German and Pronunciation.
This steamer is not one of the fastest, but a very comfortable one	Dieser Dampfer ist zwar keiner ˈdiːzər ˈdampfər ʔɪst tsvaːr ˈkaɪnər der schnellsten, aber sehr bequem der ˈʃnɛlstən ˈʔaːbər zeːr bəˈkveːm
Where does she stop on the voyage?	Wo legt das Schiff unterwegs an? voː leːkt das ʃɪf ʔuntərˈveːks ʔan?
Where is my cabin?	Wo ist meine Kabine? voː ʔɪst ˈmaɪnə kaˈbiːnə?
I can't stand the noise of the propeller	Ich kann den Lärm der Schrauben ʔɪç kan den lɛrm der ˈʃraʊbən nicht vertragen nɪçt fɛrˈtraːgən
Where can I get a deck-chair?	Wo kann ich einen Liegestuhl voː kan ʔɪç ˈʔaɪnən ˈliːgəʃtuːl mieten? ˈmiːtən?
Is there a doctor on board?	Ist ein Arzt an Bord? ʔɪst ʔaɪn ʔaːrtst ʔan bɔrt?
My wife has been seasick for some days	Meine Frau ist seit Tagen seekrank ˈmaɪnə fraʊ ʔɪst zaɪt ˈtaːgən ˈzeːkraŋk
Are you a good sailor?	Sind Sie seefest? zɪnt ziː ˈzeːfɛst?
We are having a very rough passage	Wir haben eine stürmische viːr ˈhaːbən ˈʔaɪnə ˈʃtʏrmɪʃə Überfahrt ˈʔyːbərfaːrt
The ship is rolling and pitching dreadfully	Das Schiff stampft und schlingert das ʃɪf ʃtampft ʔunt ˈʃlɪŋərt furchtbar ˈfurçtbaːr
The sea is very rough	Es ist hoher Seegang ʔɛs ʔɪst ˈhoːər ˈzeːgaŋ
It is getting foggy	Es wird nebelig ʔɛs vɪrt ˈneːbəlɪç
Visibility is bad	Wir haben sehr schlechte Sicht viːr ˈhaːbən zeːr ˈʃlɛçtə zɪçt

English.	German and Pronunciation.
The fog-horn is sounding	**Das Nebelhorn tutet**
	das ˈneːbəlhɔrn ˈtuːtət
Where can I send a wireless telegram ?	**Wo kann ich ein drahtloses Telegramm aufgeben ?**
	voː kan ʔɪç ʔaɪn ˈdraːtloːzəs teleˈgram ˈʔaʊfgeːbən ?
In the wireless-operator's cabin	**In der Funkstelle**
	ʔɪn der ˈfuŋkʃtɛlə
Get your passports and landing cards ready, please	**Alle Pässe und Landungskarten bereit halten, bitte**
	ˈʔalə ˈpɛsə ʔunt ˈlanduŋsˈkartən bəˈraɪt ˈhaltən, ˈbɪtə
We shall soon be alongside	**Wir werden bald anlegen**
	viːr ˈveɪrdən balt ˈʔanleɪgən

TRAVELLING BY AIR (LUFTREISEN)

The land area of Germany being greater than that of great Britain, nearly all towns of any size have a local aerodrome. That of Berlin is actually within the city.   Many are provided with hotel accommodation for passengers, and restaurants and gardens where refreshments are served.   Passengers are conveyed to and from the airports by a special bus service. The chief air centres are : Frankfurt, Leipzig, Berlin, Düsseldorf, Munich and Dresden.   Lufthansa is the German civil line.

Vocabulary

English.	German.	Pronunciation.
The air-transport	**der Lufttransport**	der ˈlufttransˈpɔrt
The aircraft	**das Flugzeug**	das ˈfluːktsɔʏk
The flying-boat	**das Flugboot**	das ˈfluːkboːt
The helicopter	**der Hubschrauber**	der ˈhuːpʃraʊbər
The engine	**der Motor**	der ˈmoːtɔr
The airscrew (propeller)	**die Luftschraube (der Propeller)**	di ˈluftʃraʊbə (deːr proˈpɛlər)

English.	German.	Pronunciation.
The cabin	die Kabine	di ka'bi:nə
The cockpit	der Führersitz	der 'fy:rər'zɪts
The wing	der Flügel	der 'fly:gəl
The undercarriage	das Fahrgestell	das 'fa:rgə'ʃtɛl
The airways time-table (guide)	der Flugplan	der 'flu:k'pla:n
The Continental Airways	der Europaflug-dienst	der ʔɔʏ'ro:pa'flu:k-di:nst
The passenger	der Fluggast	der 'flu:kgast
The airport	der Flughafen	der 'flu:k'ha:fən
The aerodrome	der Flugplatz	der 'flu:kplats
To take off	starten, abfliegen	'ʃta:rtən, 'ʔapfli:gən
To land	landen	'landən
To fly	fliegen	'fli:gən

Phrases

English.	German and Pronunciation.
Which is the quickest way to the aero-drome?	Wie komme ich schnellstens zum vi: 'kɔmə ʔɪç 'ʃnɛlstəns tsum Flughafen? 'flu:k'ha:fən?
When does the next plane leave for Vienna?	Wann startet das nächste Flug-van 'ʃta:rtət das 'nɛ:çstə 'flu:k-zeug nach Wien? tsɔʏk na:x vi:n?
The time-table is in the hall	Sie finden den Flugplan in der zi 'fɪndən den 'flu:kpla:n ʔɪn der Halle 'halə
I should like to travel without breaking the journey (without intermediate landing)	Ich möchte die Strecke ohne ʔɪç 'mœçtə di 'ʃtrɛkə 'ʔo:nə Zwischenlandung zurücklegen 'tsvɪʃən'landuŋ tsu'rʏkle:gən

English.	German and Pronunciation.
How many passengers does this aircraft (plane) take ?	Wieviele Fluggäste fasst diese viː'fiːlə 'fluːkgɛstə fast 'diːzə Maschine ? ma'ʃiːnə ?
This plane carries fifty passengers in the cabin and a crew of five	Dieses Flugzeug kann fünfzig 'diːzəs 'fluːktsɔʏk kan 'fʏnftsɪç Fahrgäste in der Kabine und 'faːrgɛstə ɪn der ka'biːnə ʔʊnt fünf Mann Besatzung befördern fʏnf man bə'zatsʊŋ bə'fœrdərn
Where will they put my luggage ?	Wo bringt man mein Gepäck unter ? voː brɪŋt man maɪn gə'pɛk 'ʔʊntər ?
In the luggage hold	Im Gepäckraum ʔɪm gə'pɛkraʊm
The plane is just taxi-ing out of the hangar	Das Flugzeug rollt eben aus der das 'fluːktsɔʏk rɔlt 'ʔeɪbən ʔaʊs der Halle 'halə
It is a four-engined plane	Es ist ein viermotoriges Flug- ʔɛs ʔɪst ʔaɪn 'fiːrmo'toːrɪgəs 'fluːk- zeug tsɔʏk
Europe is served by a network of air-routes	Europa besitzt ein Netz von Flug- ʔɔʏ'roːpa bə'zɪtst ʔaɪn 'nɛts fɔn 'fluːk- strecken ʃtrɛkən
The load-capacity of aircraft is limited	Die Tragfähigkeit der Flugzeuge diː 'traːkfɛːɪçkaɪt der 'fluːktsɔʏgə ist beschränkt ʔɪst bə'ʃrɛŋkt

TRAVELLING BY BICYCLE (RADFAHREN)

In Germany there are often special parts of the road-
way allocated to cyclists. This obviates danger to motorists.
Cyclists may not ride two abreast in crowded thoroughfares.
Every bicycle must have a rear-light or reflector behind,
known as a "cat's-eye" (**Katzenauge**). Motor-cycle owners
have to pass a rather stiff driving test.

Vocabulary

English.	German.	Pronunciation.
The bicycle	**das Rad, das Fahrrad**	das raɪt, das ˈfaɪrat
The handle-bar	**die Lenkstange**	di leŋkˈʃtaŋə
The saddle	**der Sattel**	der ˈzatəl
The pedal	**das Pedal**	das peˈdaːl
The free-wheel	**der Freilauf**	der ˈfraɪlauf
The chain	**die Kette**	di ˈkɛtə
The bell	**die Klingel**	di ˈklɪŋəl
The frame	**der Rahmen**	der ˈraːmən
The spokes	**die Speichen**	di ˈʃpaɪçən
The pump	**die Pumpe**	di ˈpumpə
The tool-bag	**die Werkzeugtasche**	di ˈvɛrktsɔykˈtaʃə
The back-pedalling brake	**die Rücktrittbremse**	di ˈrʏktrɪtˈbrɛmzə
The map	**die Karte**	di kaːrtə
The Youth Hostel	**die Jugendherberge**	di ˈjuːɡəntˈheːr beːrɡə

Phrases

English.	German and Pronunciation.
I am fond of cycling	**Ich radle gern. Ich fahre gern Rad** ʔɪç ˈraːdlə ɡɛrn. ʔɪç ˈfaːrə ɡɛrn raɪt
Is your brake in work-ing order ?	**Funktioniert Ihre Bremse?** fuŋktsĭoˈniːrt ˈʔiːrə ˈbrɛmzə ?
Yes, but the chain is a bit loose	**Ja, aber die Kette hat sich etwas** jaː ˈʔabər di ˈkɛtə hat zɪç ˈʔɛtvas **gelockert** ɡəˈlɔkərt

English.	German and Pronunciation.
You are riding on the pavement, you will have to pay a fine	Sie fahren auf dem Bürgersteig, Sie zi 'fa:rən ʔauf dem 'byrgər'ʃtaɪk, zi müssen Ordnungsstrafe (Geld- 'mysən 'ordnuŋs'ʃtra:fə ('gɛlt- strafe) bezahlen ʃtra:fə) bə'tsa:lən
I shall have to push my bicycle up-hill	Ich muss mein Rad bergauf ʔiç mus main ra:t bɛrk'ʔauf schieben 'ʃi:bən
I must inflate the tyres	Ich muss die Reifen aufpumpen ʔiç mus di 'raɪfən 'ʔaufpumpən
I have got a puncture in my back tyre and shall have to mend it	Ich habe ein Loch im Hinterreifen ʔiç 'ha:bə ʔain lox ʔim 'hintər'raɪfən und muss ihn flicken (ausbessern) ʔunt mus ʔi:n 'flɪkən ('ausbɛsərn)
Put your bicycle into the shed	Stellen Sie Ihr Rad unter 'ʃtɛlən zi ʔi:r rait 'ʔuntər
No cycling	Radfahren verboten ! 'ra:tfa:rən fɛr'bo:tən !

THE TOWN (DIE STADT)

There are more apartment-houses or blocks of flats in Germany than in England. Most streets in the modern parts of a town are lined with trees. In Germany the principal means of transport is the tramcar, but the number of motor-buses is increasing. Only the biggest towns (Hamburg, Berlin) have underground railways.

Vocabulary

English.	German.	Pronunciation.
The town, city	die Stadt	di ʃtat
The capital	die Hauptstadt	di 'hauptʃtat
The suburb	der Vorort	der 'fo:rʔort

English.	German.	Pronunciation.
The market-square	der Marktplatz	der ˈmarktplats
The street	die Strasse	di ˈʃtraːsə
The lane	die Gasse	di ˈgasə
The main street	die Hauptstrasse	di ˈhauptʃtraːsə
The side street	die Seitenstrasse	di ˈzaɪtənˈʃtraːsə
The street corner	die Strassenecke	di ˈʃtraːsenˈʔɛkə
The crossing	die Strassen- kreuzung	di ˈʃtraːsən- ˈkrɔʏtsuŋ
The roadway	der Fahrdamm	der ˈfaːrdam
The pavement	der Bürgersteig	der ˈbʏrgərˈʃtaɪk
The gardens	die Anlagen	di ˈanlaːgən
The bridge	die Brücke	di ˈbrʏkə
The cemetery	der Friedhof	der ˈfriːthoːf
The building	das Gebäude	das gəˈbɔydə
The hospital	das Krankenhaus	das ˈkraŋkənˈhaus
The town hall	das Rathaus	das ˈraːthaus
The post-office	die Post, das Postamt	di pɔst, das ˈpɔstʔamt
The police station	die Polizei, das Polizeirevier	di poliˈtsaɪ, das poliˈtsaɪreˈviːr
The policeman	der Schutzmann, der Polizist	der ˈʃutsman, der poliˈtsɪst
The public library	die Stadtbibliothek, die Stadtbücherei	di ˈʃtatbiblioˈteːk, di ˈʃtatbyːçəˈraɪ
The school	die Schule, das Schulgebäude	di ˈʃuːlə, das ˈʃuːlgəˈbɔydə
The church	die Kirche	di ˈkɪrçə
The university	die Universität	di ʔunɪvɛrziˈtɛːt
The cathedral	der Dom	der doːm
The fire station	die Feuerwache	di ˈfɔyərˈvaxə
The block of flats	das Mietshaus	das ˈmiːtshaus
The public house	die Kneipe, die Wirtschaft	di ˈknaɪpə, di ˈvɪrtʃaft
The restaurant	das Restaurant	das rɛstoˈrãː
The shop	der Laden das Geschäft	der ˈlaːdən das gəˈʃɛft

English.	German.	Pronunciation.
The shop window	das Schaufenster	das ˈʃaufɛnstər
The pedestrian	der Fussgänger	der ˈfuːsgɛŋər
The tramcar	die Strassenbahn, die Elektrische	di ˈʃtraːsənˈbaːn, di ɐeˈlɛktrɪʃə
The underground	die Untergrundbahn (U-Bahn)	di ˈʔuntərgrunt-ˈbaːn (ˈʔuːbaːn)
The bus	der Autobus, der Omnibus	der ˈʔautobus, der ˈʔɔmnibus
The lorry	das Lastauto	das ˈlastʔautoː
The stopping place	die Haltestelle	di ˈhaltəˈʃtɛlə
The terminus	die Endstation	di ˈʔɛntʃtatsiˈoːn

Phrases

English.	German and Pronunciation.
How far is it to the High Street ?	Wie weit ist es zur Haupt-strasse ? viː vait ʔist ʔəs tsur ˈhaupt-ʃtraːsə ?
Which is the quickest way to the cathedral ?	Wie komme ich am schnellsten zum Dom ? viː ˈkɔmə ʔiç ʔam ˈʃnɛlstən tsum ˈdoːm ?
Can you tell me the way to the theatre ?	Können Sie mir den Weg zum Theater sagen (zeigen) ? ˈkœnən zi miːr den veːk tsum teˈaːtər ˈzaːgən (ˈtsaigən) ?
Where is the post-office ?	Wo ist die Post ? voː ʔist di pɔst ?
The second turning on the right	Die zweite Strasse rechts di ˈtsvaitə ˈʃtraːsə rɛçts
Don't cross the street unless the green light is on	Sie dürfen die Strasse nur bei grünem Licht überqueren zi ˈdʏrfən di ˈʃtraːsə nuːr bai ˈgryːnəm lɪçt ʔyːbərˈkveːrən

English.	German and Pronunciation.
There are the traffic lights	**Dort ist die Verkehrsampel**
	dɔrt ʔɪst di fɛrˈkeirsʔampəl
Don't step off the pavement	**Gehen Sie nicht vom Bürgersteig**
	ˈgeiən zi nɪçt fɔm ˈbyrgərˈʃtaɪk
	herunter
	hɛˈrʊntər
The traffic is very heavy	**Es ist sehr starker Verkehr**
	ʔes ʔɪst zeir ˈʃtarkər fɛrˈkeir
The streets are too narrow	**Die Strassen sind zu eng**
	di ˈʃtraɪsən zɪnt tsuɪ ʔɛŋ
I have lost my way	**Ich habe mich verlaufen**
	ʔɪç ˈhaɪbə mɪç fɛrˈlaufən
Turn to the left	**Links einbiegen !**
	lɪŋks ʔˈaɪnbiigən !
Straight on	**Geradeaus !**
	gəˈraɪdəʔˈaus !
Where is the main entrance to the hospital?	**Wo ist der Haupteingang zum**
	voɪ ʔɪst der ˈhauptʔaɪngaŋ tsʊm
	Krankenhaus?
	ˈkraŋkənˈhaus ?
Where does Mr. Smith live?	**Wo wohnt Herr Schmidt ?**
	voɪ voint hɛr ʃmɪt ?
On the top floor	**Im obersten Stock**
	ʔɪm ˈʔoɪbərstən ʃtɔk
They have a flat on the ground floor	**Sie haben eine Wohnung (Etage)**
	zi ˈhaɪbən ʔˈaɪnə ˈvoinuŋ (ʔeˈtaɪʒə)
	im Erdgeschoss
	ʔɪm ʔˈeirtgəˈʃɔs
Can I get to the Palacesquare by underground?	**Kann ich mit der Untergrund**
	kan ʔɪç mit der ʔˈʔʊntərgrʊnt
	bahn nach dem Schlossplatz
	baɪn naɪx dem ˈʃlɔsplats
	kommen ?
	ˈkɔmən ?

English.	German and Pronunciation.
Take the escalator. Or do you prefer the stairs ?	**Nehmen Sie die Rolltreppe ! Oder** ˈneːmən ziː diː ˈrɔltrɛpə. ˈʔoːdər **ziehen Sie die Treppe vor ?** ˈtsiːən ziː diː ˈtrɛpə foːr ?
You have to book a ticket	**Sie müssen eine Karte lösen** ziː ˈmʏsən ˈʔaɪnə ˈkartə ˈløːzən
Take your tickets from the machines	**Ziehen Sie die Karten an dem** ˈtsiːən ziː diː ˈkartən ˈʔan dem **Automaten !** ʔautoˈmaːtən !
You can also take the bus	**Sie können auch den Omnibus** ziː ˈkœnən ʔaux den ˈʔɔmnibʊs **nehmen** ˈneːmən
Does this bus take me to the park ?	**Fährt der Omnibus (Autobus) nach** ˈfɛːrt der ˈɔmnibʊs (ˈʔautobʊs) naːx **dem Park?** dem park ?
The buses are crowded	**Die Omnibusse sind überfüllt** diː ˈʔɔmnibʊsə zɪnt ʔyːbərˈfʏlt
We are full up. Take the next bus, please	**Besetzt. Nehmen Sie den nächsten** bəˈzɛtst. ˈneːmən ziː den ˈnɛːçstən **(Omnibus) !** (ˈʔɔmnibʊs) !
No room on top, standing-room inside only	**Oben alles voll, unten nur** ˈʔoːbən ˈʔaləs ˈfɔl, ˈʔʊntən nuːr **Stehplätze !** ˈʃteːplɛtsə !
Don't push	**Nicht drängen !** nɪçt ˈdrɛŋən !
Fares, please	**Bitte, das Fahrgeld ! Bitte schön !** ˈbɪtə, das ˈfaːrgɛlt ! ˈbɪtə ʃøːn !
Move up, please	**Bitte nach vorne durchgehen !** ˈbɪtə naːx fɔrnə ˈdʊrçgeːən !
Keep a passage clear	**Den Gang freilassen !** den gaŋ ˈfraɪlasən !

English.	German and Pronunciation.
I have lost my ticket	**Ich habe meinen Fahrschein verloren** ʔɪç ˈhaːbə ˈmaɪnən ˈfaɪrʃaɪn fɛrˈloɪrən
A transfer to the Central Station	**Eine Umsteigekarte nach dem** ˈʔaɪnə ˈʔumʃtaɪgəˈkartə naːx dem **Hauptbahnhof** ˈhauptbaɪnˈhoːf
Don't alight when the vehicle is in motion	**Während der Fahrt nicht abspringen !** ˈvɛˈrənt der faːrt nɪçt ˈʔapʃprɪŋən !
When does the last metropolitan train leave?	**Wann fährt die letzte Stadtbahn ?** van fɛɪrt di ˈlɛtstə ˈʃtatbaɪn ?
Sunday traffic is limited	**Der Sonntagsverkehr ist einge-** der ˈzɔntaːksfɛrˈkeːr ʔɪst ˈʔaɪngə- **schränkt** ˈʃrɛŋkt
Where do I have to get off?	**Wo muss ich aussteigen ?** voː mus ʔɪç ˈʔausʃtaɪgən ?
No thoroughfare for vehicles	**Für Fahrzeuge gesperrt !** fyr ˈfaːrtsɔʏgə gəˈʃpɛrt !
Closed to pedestrians	**Für Fussgänger gesperrt !** fyr ˈfuːsgɛŋər gəˈʃpɛrt !
No admittance (private)	**Eintritt verboten !** ˈʔaɪntrɪt fɛrˈboːtən !

HOTELS

As in most countries there are hotels of various classes in Germany: the luxury or first-class hotels (**Hotels ersten Ranges**), the second- and third-class hotels (**Hotels zweiten und dritten Ranges**). The good ones are recommended by the German **Automobilklub** (**ADAC**) or are starred in the guide-books (**Reiseführer**). There are no temperance hotels in Germany. They are all licensed (**sie haben Schankkon-zession**). Although in principle tipping (**Trinkgeld**) has been abolished and replaced by a ten to fifteen per cent. surcharge on the bill, waiters will not be found to refuse tips when proffered. In many villages and small towns not usually frequented by travellers the inns (**Gasthäuser**) and small hotels are rather primitive. Boarding-houses (**Pensionen**) are mostly confined to the larger towns and health and summer resorts. There bed and breakfast (**ein Zimmer mit Frühstück**) can also be obtained.

Vocabulary

English.	German.	Pronunciation.
The inn, guest-house	das Gasthaus	das ˈgasthaʊs
The single room	das Einzelzimmer	das ˈʔaɪntsəlˈtsɪmər
The double room	das Zimmer mit zwei Betten	das ˈtsɪmər mɪt tsvaɪ ˈbɛtən
The reception desk	das Empfangs-büro	das ʔɛmˈpfaŋs-byˈroː
The lounge	die Hotelhalle	di hoˈtɛlhalə
The public rooms	die Gesellschafts-räume	di gəˈzɛlʃafts-ˈrɔymə
The dining-room	der Speisesaal	der ˈʃpaɪzəˈzaːl
The writing-room	das Schreibzimmer	das ˈʃraɪptsɪmər
The gentlemen's cloak-room	die Herrentoilette	di ˈhɛrəntoaˈlɛtə
The ladies' cloak-room	die Damentoilette	di ˈdaːməntoaˈlɛtə
The bell	die Klingel	di ˈklɪŋəl
The bell-boy (page)	der Page	der ˈpaːʒə
The chambermaid	das Zimmermäd-chen	das ˈtsɪmərˈmɛːt-çən
The boots	der Stiefelputzer, der Hoteldiener	der ˈʃtiːfəlˈpʊtsər, der hoˈtɛldiːnər
The waiter	der Kellner	der ˈkɛlnər
The head waiter	der Oberkellner	der ˈʔoːbərˈkɛlnər
The waitress	die Kellnerin	di ˈkɛlnərɪn
The porter	der Portier	der portiˈeː
The manager	der Hoteldirektor	der hoˈtɛldiˈrɛktɔr
The proprietor	der Besitzer	der bəˈzɪtsər

Phrases

English.	German and Pronunciation.
At which hotel are you staying?	In welchem Hotel halten Sie sich ʔɪn ˈvɛlçəm hoˈtɛl ˈhaltən zi ziç auf? ʔauf?
The service is good (bad)	Die Bedienung ist gut (schlecht) di bəˈdiːnuŋ ʔɪst guːt (ʃlɛçt)
Can I have a single room looking out over the park?	Können Sie mir ein Einzelzimmer ˈkœnən zi miːr ʔaɪn ˈʔaɪntsəlˈtsɪmər mit Aussicht auf den Park geben? mɪt ˈʔauszɪçt ʔaufden park ˈgeːbən?
Is there central-heating and running water in the rooms?	Haben die Zimmer Zentralheizung ˈhaːbən di ˈtsɪmər tsenˈtraːlhaɪtsuŋ und fliessendes Wasser? ʔunt ˈfliːsəndəs ˈvasər?
Here is the key to your room	Hier ist der Zimmerschlüssel hiːr ʔɪst der ˈtsɪmərˈʃlʏsəl
The lift-boy will take your luggage up	Der Liftjunge wird Ihr Gepäck der ˈlɪftjuŋə vɪrt ʔiːr gəˈpɛk hinaufbringen hɪˈnaufbrɪŋən
Can I have breakfast in my room?	Kann ich das Frühstück auf dem kan ʔɪç das ˈfryːʃtʏk ʔauf dem Zimmer haben? ˈtsɪmər ˈhaːbən?
Where is the bar?	Wo ist die Bar? voː ʔɪst di baːr?
Where is the bathroom, please?	Bitte, wo ist das Badezimmer? ˈbɪtə voː ʔɪst das ˈbaːdəˈtsɪmər?
Please enter your name and address in the visitors' book	Bitte, schreiben Sie Namen und ˈbɪtə ˈʃraɪbən zi ˈnaːmən ʔunt Adresse in das Fremdenbuch ʔaˈdrɛsə ʔɪn das ˈfrɛmdənˈbuːx
How long do you intend to stay?	Wie lange gedenken Sie zu bleiben? viː ˈlaŋə gəˈdɛŋkən zi tsu ˈblaɪbən?

English.	German and Pronunciation.
What are your inclusive terms?	Was rechnen Sie für Pension? vas ˈrɛçnən zi fyr pãsĭˈoːn?
I want to lodge a complaint with the manager	Ich möchte mich beim Hoteldirektor ʔɪç ˈmœçtə mɪç baɪm hoˈtɛldiˈrɛktɔr beschweren bəˈʃveːrən
How much is bed and breakfast?	Was kostet das Zimmer mit Früh- vas ˈkɔstət das ˈtsɪmər mɪt ˈfryː- stück? ʃtʏk?
I should like another blanket or a quilt	Ich hätte gern noch eine Wolldecke ʔɪç ˈhɛtə gɛrn nɔx ˈʔaɪnə ˈvɔldɛkə oder eine Daunendecke ˈʔoːdər ˈʔaɪnə ˈdaʊnənˈdɛkə
Please give me another towel and some soap	Bitte geben Sie mir noch ein Hand- ˈbɪtə ˈgeːbən zi miːr nɔx ʔaɪn ˈhant- tuch und ein Stück Seife tuːx ʔʊnt ʔaɪn ʃtʏk ˈzaɪfə
Can you call me to-morrow at six o'clock?	Können Sie mich morgen früh um ˈkœnən zi mɪç ˈmɔrgən fryː ʔʊm sechs wecken? zɛks ˈvɛkən?
I have ordered a room with bath	Ich habe ein Zimmer mit Bad ʔɪç ˈhaːbə ʔaɪn ˈtsɪmər mɪt baːt bestellt bəˈʃtɛlt
Have you reserved a room for me?	Haben Sie mir ein Zimmer reser- ˈhaːbən zi miːr ʔaɪn ˈtsɪmər rezɛr- viert? ˈviːrt?
Any letters for me?	Sind Briefe für mich da? zɪnt ˈbriːfə fyr mɪç daː?
Ring twice for the chambermaid	Nach dem Zimmermädchen zweimal naːx dem ˈtsɪmərˈmɛːtçən ˈtsvaɪmaːl klingeln! ˈklɪŋəln!

English.	German and Pronunciation.
Where did you put my comb and brush ?	Wo haben Sie Kamm und Bürste vo: 'ha:bən zi kam ʔʊnt 'bʏrstə hingelegt ? 'hɪngə'le:kt ?
When can you let me have my laundry ?	Wann kann ich meine Wäsche van kan ʔɪç 'maɪnə 'vɛʃə zurückhaben ? tsu'rʏkha:bən ?

Laundry List :   *Wäschezettel* ('vɛʃə'tsɛtəl) :

Four white shirts	Vier weisse Hemden fi:r 'vaɪsə 'hɛmdən
Three coloured shirts	Drei bunte Hemden draɪ 'bʊntə 'hɛmdən
Six stiff collars	Sechs steife Kragen zɛks 'ʃtaɪfə 'kra:gən
Five soft collars	Fünf weiche Kragen fʏnf 'vaɪçə 'kra:gən
Two vests	Zwei Unterhemden tsvaɪ 'ʔʊntər'hɛmdən
Two pairs of under-pants	Zwei Paar Unterhosen tsvaɪ pa:r 'ʔʊntər'ho:zən
One pair of pyjamas	Ein Schlafanzug ʔaɪn 'ʃla:f'ʔantsu:k
One nightdress (night-gown)	Ein Nachthemd ʔaɪn 'naxthɛmt
Ten handkerchiefs	Zehn Taschentücher tse:n 'taʃən'ty:çər
Five pairs of socks (stockings)	Fünf Paar Socken (Strümpfe) fʏnf pa:r 'zɔkən ('ʃtrʏmpfə)
One slip	Ein Unterkleid ʔaɪn 'ʔʊntər'klaɪt
Three camiknickers	Drei Hemdhosen draɪ 'hɛmt'ho:zən

English.	German and Pronunciation.
Two blouses	**Zwei Blusen** tsvaɪ ˈbluːzən
One linen dress	**Ein Leinenkleid** ʔaɪn ˈlaɪnənˈklaɪt
I have forgotten my safety razor	**Ich habe meinen Rasierapparat** ʔɪç ˈhaːbə ˈmaɪnən raˈziːrʔapaˈraːt **vergessen** fərˈgɛsən
Is there a barber's shop in the hotel?	**Ist ein Friseur im Hotel?** ʔɪst ʔaɪn friˈzøːr ʔɪm hoˈtɛl?
Can you have this suit pressed for me?	**Können Sie diesen Anzug zum** ˈkœnən ziː ˈdiːzən ˈʔantsuːk tsʊm **Aufbügeln schicken?** ˈʔaʊfbyːgəln ˈʃɪkən?
Let me have the bill, please	**Die Rechnung, bitte!** diː ˈrɛçnʊŋ, ˈbɪtə
Do you like your boarding-house?	**Sind Sie mit Ihrer Pension zu-** ˈzɪnt ziː mɪt ˈʔiːrər ˈpãsiˈoːn tsu- **frieden?** ˈfriːdən?
The food is good and plentiful	**Das Essen ist gut und reichlich** das ˈʔɛsən ʔɪst guːt ʔʊnt ˈraɪçlɪç
The cooking is excellent	**Die Küche ist ausgezeichnet** diː ˈkʏçə ʔɪst ʔaʊsgəˈtsaɪçnət
Can I book rooms for August?	**Kann ich Zimmer für August** kan ʔɪç ˈtsɪmər fyr ʔaʊˈgʊst **bestellen?** bəˈʃtɛlən?
Sorry, we are booked till October	**Leider nichts frei vor Oktober** ˈlaɪdər nɪçts fraɪ foːr ʔɔkˈtoːbər

RESTAURANTS AND MEALS
(RESTAURANTS UND MAHLZEITEN)

People frequent restaurants in Germany more than in England, and many men have their regularly reserved tables which are known as **Stammtische**. Those restaurants where meals and only beer are served are called **Bräu**, usually under the name of the particular brew of beer which they serve (**ausschenken**), for instance **Löwenbräu, Patzenhofer, Schultheiss,** etc. All the cafés and most of the restaurants provide newspapers and periodicals for the benefit of their customers. Many cafés and restaurants have a garden attached. In the country they are usually called **Biergarten**. In Germany the main meal is taken at midday.

Vocabulary

English.	German.	Pronunciation.
The plate	**der Teller**	der ˈtɛlər
The dish	**die Schüssel, das Gericht**	di ˈʃʏsəl, das gəˈrɪçt
The knife	**das Messer**	das ˈmɛsər
The fork	**die Gabel**	di ˈgaːbəl
The spoon	**der Löffel**	der ˈlœfəl
The cup	**die Tasse**	di ˈtasə
The saucer	**die Untertasse**	di ˈʔuntərˈtasə
The glass	**das Glas**	das glaːs
The tea-pot	**die Teekanne**	di ˈteːkanə
The coffee-pot	**die Kaffeekanne**	di ˈkafeːˈkanə
The milk jug	**die Milchkanne, der Milchtopf**	di ˈmɪlçkanə, der ˈmɪlçtɔpf
The sugar-basin	**die Zuckerdose**	di ˈtsukərˈdoːzə
The tray	**das Tablett**	das taˈblɛt
The breakfast	**das Frühstück**	das ˈfryːʃtʏk
The lunch	**das Mittagessen**	das ˈmɪtaːkʔɛsən